# Feeling Good About Yourself

## Strategies to Guide Young People Toward More Positive, Personal Feelings

**by
Debbie Pincus**

**illustrated by Judy Hierstein**

Cover by Judy Hierstein

Copyright © Good Apple, Inc., 1990

ISBN No. 0-86653-516-0

**Good Apple**
A Division of Frank Schaffer Publications, Inc.
23740 Hawthorne Boulevard
Torrance, CA 90505-5927

# To the Memories

Dedicated to the memories of my dad, Dr. William Pincus, my fiancé, Mark Lasky, and my dear friend, Laura Penn-Bourget.

# Acknowledgement

To my husband, Richard Ward, my mother, Reva Pincus, my sister, Arlyne Eisberg, and my niece and nephew, Scott and Lindsay Eisberg, and my many wonderful friends. Having them in my life has helped me to feel good about myself.

GA1139

# About the Author

Debbie Pincus is the Director of Counseling at the College of Mount Saint Vincent, the Director of Behavioral Counseling at the Physicians Smoke Stopping Center and a psychotherapist in private practice in New York City. She designed and implemented the Interpersonal Communications Program in many public and private schools. Ms. Pincus leads workshops and seminars on effective communication, which have received national recognition, and she has been selected for inclusion in Who's Who Among Human Service Professionals. She is the author of the books *Sharing* and *Interactions* published by Good Apple, Inc.

GA1139

# Table of Contents

GA1139

# Introduction

Rational-Emotive Therapy was developed in 1955 by internationally recognized psychologist Albert Ellis. Dr. Ellis was a practicing psychoanalyst who became frustrated with the slow progress made by his patients and searched the literature of the ancient Greek and Roman philosophers for more efficient methods. He discovered the work of Epictatus who stated that it was not events that disturbed men but their view of these events. This became the cornerstone of RET. He then proceeded to develop an active, directive approach to therapy which teaches individuals to recognize that their self-defeating emotions are the result of irrational thoughts. Rigid, absolutistic beliefs are at the core of emotional disturbance. He created an approach to behavior change which teaches individuals to dispute these rigid, absolutistic thoughts.

In 1959, Dr. Ellis founded the Institute for Rational Living, a nonprofit educational organization and in 1968, the Institute for Rational-Emotive Therapy was founded to provide professional training and counseling services. Today the two institutes are merged into one comprehensive multiservice facility housed in a beautiful turn-of-the century town house in the upper Eastside of New York City. At present an estimated ten thousand psychologists, psychiatrists, social workers and counselors are using RET throughout the world. The New York Institute currently has affiliates in Cleveland, Clearwater, Charlottesville, Philadelphia, Dallas, Denver, Portland and Southern California. In addition, affiliates exist outside the U.S. in Australia, England, Germany, Italy, Mexico, and the Netherlands.

Rational Effectiveness Training Systems, the corporate services division of the Institute, offers training to business and industry to improve the productivity of employees and increase managerial effectiveness.

*Feeling Good About Yourself* is an excellent book for young people who want to learn how to manage their emotions and live a happy and productive life. It will be very useful as the foundation to any emotional education program.

Dominic J. Di Mattia, Ed.D
Virginia and Harvey Hubbel     and
Professor of Counseling
University of Bridgeport

Director of Corporate Services
Institute for Rational-Emotive
Therapy, NYC

GA1139

# Thinking Straight and Feeling Good

## For the Teacher

The exercises in this chapter will help the students understand how one's thinking about an event will produce feelings. They will learn that they feel the way they think. The goal will be for students to recognize inaccuracies in their thinking and arrive at a more realistic view of themselves and their surroundings.

Teach the students the A-B-C-D-E model as described below.

A. (Event) I get rejected

B. (Beliefs or Thoughts)
I can't take it.
She has no right.
It's a horrible situation.
I'm worthless.
I'll never be liked by anyone.

C. (Emotional Reaction)
Depressed, angry, cried, couldn't eat, fought with my sister.

Explain to the students that this person's beliefs about the event are examples of irrational thinking. They would lead anyone to be unhappy and upset. Explain that a rejection may have practical disadvantages, but it need not be considered a catastrophe. Only one's point of view can do that. The kind of ideas that cause people to get upset and lead to unhappiness usually have one or two words in common: AWFUL and SHOULD. Explain to the students that AWFUL includes a host of attitudinal exaggerations and extremes such as *terrible, horrible* or *dreadful.* SHOULD includes such attitudinal absolutes as *must, ought, got, need, insist.* It's the attitude behind the words that causes the problems. SHOULD is usually an unrealistic demand. Teach students to dispute these SHOULDS and AWFULS by asking WHY? Why is it awful? Where is my proof? The student may discover that a particular situation may be unfortunate or highly unpleasant with realistic disadvantages, but it is unlikely that anything is truly terrible or horrible. Students will need to add D and E to the model above to do this successfully. D means to dispute, question, challenge. Using the above example, why can't you take it? Why does being rejected make you worthless? Why is it so horrible? E is most important. It is at this point where the WHYS are answered. Why does being rejected make you worthless? It doesn't. It may be disappointing or upsetting, but no one is worthless. You are obviously worthy in many ways and to many people. Where do you get the idea that everyone must accept you? That's an unrealistic expectation.

Ask students to think of events in their own lives that caused them irrational beliefs and emotional reactions. Ask them to dispute their beliefs by asking why to the SHOULDS and AWFULS and answering the whys with more rational beliefs.

The students are now ready to begin the chapter. Each activity should be followed by class discussion.

GA1139

# Responsibility

Responsibility is_____

I am most **R**esponsible when _____

I f**E**el most responsible to _____

Being responsible make**S** me feel_____

I believe that being res**P**onsible means_____

When **O**ther people are responsible to me, I feel _____

When others are respo**N**sible to me, they do_____

The re**S**ponsibilities that I enjoy include_____

The respons**I**bilities that I dislike include_____

Responsi**B**ilities that I feel hard to carry include _____

What **I**'d like to be more responsible for is_____

What I'd **L**ike to be less responsible for is _____

Being respons**I**ble is/is not important to learn because _____

**T**oo many people are not responsible enough for _____

Discuss **Y**our answers with your teachers, classmates and family.

GA1139

# Chapter 1
# How to Be Responsible for Feeling Good
## Using the R.E.T. Method

GA1139

# Word Puzzle

Go on a scavenger hunt. See if you can find the following words in this chapter and underline them in red. Then look in your dictionary for each word's definition. Make sure to look up any other words that you do not know the meanings of.

sensible _____

responsible _____

emotions _____

reactions _____

baffle _____

agonized _____

enraged _____

accurate _____

indifferent _____

realistic _____

reject _____

exaggerate _____

attitudes _____

prestigious _____

challenge _____

unbearable _____

inferior _____

audition _____

evaluate _____

perplexed _____

logical _____

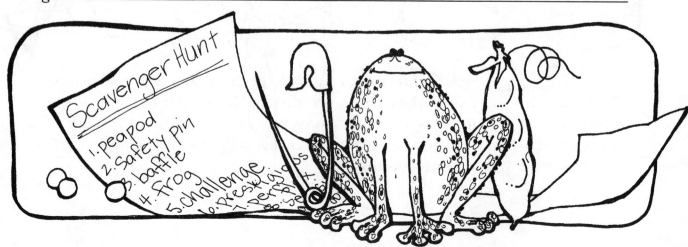

GA1139

# Check Off

What causes you, your friends, family and people in general to feel upset, angry, disturbed or any of the other various emotions? Check off all the possible causes below.

- ☑ Failing a test
- ☐ A friend moving away
- ☐ Someone getting sick
- ☐ Losing a job
- ☑ A friend rejecting you
- ☑ Not making the team
- ☑ Getting yelled at by a parent or teacher
- ☐ Not getting a gift you were hoping for
- ☐ Not getting a part in the play
- ☐ Losing an audition
- ☑ Getting the best grade on a test
- ☑ Winning an award
- ☐ Getting no allowance
- ☐ None of the above

None of the above events can cause us to have feelings or emotional reactions. So if you put no checks above, you are correct. Believe it or not, an event, a situation or another person cannot cause you your feelings. So who or what is responsible for how you feel? The next few activities will help you find the answer to this baffling question.

GA1139

# Detective Play

You are now a detective trying to find the answer to the question: WHAT OR WHO IS RESPONSIBLE FOR HOW WE FEEL? Ask ten different people you know (friends, family, teachers, etc.) how they would feel if they were in the following situation. Tell each person to choose a feeling word on the following page that comes closest to describing how he or she would feel and write that word below next to the person's name.

You try out for a part in a school play. You want this part very much. Your best friend gets the part. How do you feel?

Person 1 _____

Person 2 _____

Person 3 _____

Person 4 _____

Person 5 _____

Person 6 _____

Person 7 _____

Person 8 _____

Person 9 _____

Person 10 _____

What did you observe and learn from this survey? Use the information you learned to help you with the next activity.

GA11139

# Feeling Words

disgusted

indifferent

jealous

confident

sympathetic

agonized

grateful

curious

loving

apologetic

frustrated

suspicious

miserable

satisfied

shocked

enraged

disappointed

hurt

bored

happy

anxious

sad

lonely

determined

guilty

relieved

frightened

perplexed

 GA1139

# Putting It All Together

Answer the following questions based on the information you gathered from your survey.

Did each person you surveyed have the same reaction to the same situation?

_____

What do you think caused people to have different feelings and reactions to the same exact situation?

_____

Is it the situation/event that caused the feelings or is it each person's belief and attitude toward the event/situation? Explain.

_____

**********************************************************************

We are each responsible for how we feel. As you can see, the same event can cause one person to feel sad and another person to feel excited and yet another person to feel scared. It is not the event at all but rather the beliefs and attitudes we have about the event.

Write down your beliefs and attitudes about the following event:

You are not invited to a birthday party that most of your classmates are invited to.

| **Beliefs** | **Attitudes** |
| --- | --- |
| _____ | _____ |
| _____ | _____ |
| _____ | _____ |
| _____ | _____ |
| _____ | _____ |

Discuss with your teacher and classmates the feelings your own thoughts and opinions caused you. Write your feeling below.

Feeling _____

_____

_____

_____

_____

GA1139

# Finding Feeling Faces

Cut out from the cartoon section of a magazine expressions of people that would accurately describe how you might feel if you were in the following situations. Paste the pictures on the boxes.

Situation:    You do not get picked for the team that you very much wanted to be on.

Feeling:

Situation:    You get all A's on your report card.
Feeling:

Situation:    Your best friend moves away.
Feeling:

Situation:    You win a prestigious award.
Feeling:

Remember, the situation itself is not responsible for how you feel. Your own thoughts, opinions, beliefs, and attitudes are what cause you to feel what you do. The following activity will help you to understand your beliefs which caused you the feelings about the situations above.

GA1139

# Discovering My Beliefs and Attitudes

Write down all your attitudes and beliefs about each situation. Then write the feeling word that you described with pictures in the last activity.

Situation:     You do not get picked for the team that you very much wanted to be on.

My beliefs:    Example: I'm a real loser.

_____

_____

_____

My beliefs caused me to feel: _____

Situation:     You get all A's on your report card.

My beliefs:    Example: Now my parents will finally take me seriously.

_____

_____

_____

My beliefs caused me to feel: _____

Situation:     Your best friend moves away.

My beliefs:    Example: Why did this have to happen to me?

_____

_____

_____

My beliefs caused me to feel: _____

Situation:     You win a prestigious award.

My beliefs:    Example: I am special.

_____

_____

_____

My beliefs caused me to feel: _____

Discuss with your teacher and classmates how you are responsible for how you feel about a situation. A situation does not CAUSE your feelings.

GA1139

# Taking Responsibility

You want to feel content and satisfied. You are responsible for how you feel, and you know the way you choose to think about a situation affects how you feel. Circle the kinds of beliefs about the following situation that would help you to feel content and satisfied.

Event:      You have an argument with a friend.

Beliefs:    I should never fight with a friend.
            It is horrible that Cindy and I disagreed.
            We will probably never be friends again.
            The argument was not pleasant, but I'll get through it.
            It's not fair that she always picks on me.
            She deserved what she got.
            Disagreements are normal parts of relationships.
            When we make up and understand what happened, we can be even closer friends.
            She'll probably tell everyone what happened.

Feeling:    content and satisfied

_____

Write three beliefs about the following situation that would cause you the feelings listed below.

Event:      I have to take a math test tomorrow.

Beliefs:    _____

            _____

            _____

Feelings:   confident, encouraged

Discuss with your teacher and classmates how accurate beliefs instead of exaggerated beliefs (awful, horrible, should) help you to feel good.

GA1139

# It Shouldn't Be Awful!

Can you find the common characteristic in each person's beliefs and attitudes, causing the people to feel lousy?

Situation:              Your class trip gets cancelled.
John's belief:          That is terrible!
Sue's belief:           That is not fair! Trips should not be cancelled.
Jason's belief:         We shouldn't have to suffer because a teacher gets ill.
Lindsay's belief:       I can't handle this. I was looking forward to today.
Scott's belief:         This is awful!

Almost all misery-producing ideas have one or two words in common. They are SHOULD and AWFUL.

AWFUL includes exaggerations and extremes such as *horrible*, *terrible*, *dreadful*. The attitude behind AWFUL is usually an unrealistic exaggeration. Disappointments become disasters.

SHOULD includes *musts*, *oughts*, *need* and *insist*. It is not the words but the attitude behind the words that causes the problems. The attitude behind SHOULD is almost always an unrealistic demand. It means I must have things my way, and I must have what I want when I want it.

Circle the words that are exaggerations in red.
Circle the words that are demands in green.

Discuss with your teacher and classmates ways in which John, Sue, Jason, Lindsay and Scott each made their unfortunate situation a disaster. Discuss the attitudes and beliefs behind the words.

10

GA1139

# The Challenge to the Rescue

Now it is time to challenge the attitudes and beliefs that cause us to feel lousy. Let's go back to the cancelled class trip that John, Sue, Jason, Lindsay and Scott feel awful about. You can challenge their beliefs by asking WHY? Why is it awful? Where is the proof? Why should it be? Who said so?

Situation:       Your class trip gets cancelled.

John:            That is terrible!

Challenger:      Why is that terrible? Where is the proof that it is terrible? This situation might be unfortunate or unpleasant, but it is not likely that it is truly terrible or horrible. Realistically it simply may have disadvantages.

Sue:             Yes, but it is not fair. Trips should not be cancelled.

Challenger:      Who said things are always fair or trips can never be cancelled? Why should things always be fair or go the way you want them to? Nothing has to be the way you want, and although it might be better if things were the way you want, that doesn't mean they MUST, OUGHT or SHOULD be that way.

Scott:           Yes, but this situation is really awful for us.

Challenger:      Frustrating situations might cause you to be very emotional, but you do not have to flip out, get panic-stricken or fly off the handle. Disadvantages and inconveniences are a reality we must live with, but awfulness and terribleness are exaggerations that we make up in our own heads.

Jason:           Yes, but we shouldn't have to suffer because a teacher gets ill.

Challenger:      Reality is reality, not what you want it to be. You are not owed satisfactions like love, approval, getting what you want all the time even if you've had many disadvantages in your life. You do not run the universe and things do not have to go your way.

Lindsay:         Yes, but I can't handle this. I was looking forward to today.

Challenger:      How is it that you can't handle this? Why not? What can't you do? What can you do to cope? Who said you must always have what you look forward to? It would be nice and probably feels disappointing, but it is not unbearable.

Discuss with your teacher and classmates how you feel having some of these attitudes and beliefs challenged? Do you want to argue or agree with the challenger? Have all the classmates who want to argue the challenger stand on one side of the room and all classmates who want to agree with the challenger on the other. Debate your ideas.

11

# Why?

AWFULS and SHOULDS lead to self-blaming and self-downing. They lead to not liking yourself. Now that you've learned to ask WHY to your attitudes of AWFUL and SHOULD, you must learn to answer the WHYS accurately as step E illustrates.

A. Situation
   You make a mistake at the assembly.

B. Attitudes and beliefs
   It's terrible that I made a mistake.
   I should never have made such a silly mistake.
   I am a real jerk for making such a stupid error.

C. Feelings (caused by your thoughts)
   Hurt
   Worthless
   Embarrassed
   Inferior

D. Dispute or challenge by asking why.
   Why is it awful that I made a mistake?
   Why shouldn't I have made the mistake?
   Why does making a mistake make me a jerk?

E. Logically and sensibly answer the whys.
   Why is it awful that I made a mistake? It is not awful. It is frustrating, but it is not the end of the world. Therefore, there is no sense stretching it into an awful situation.

   Why shouldn't I have made a mistake? It would be better if I did not make mistakes, but there is no proof that I must absolutely never make a mistake. My SHOULD is a demand that I be perfect.

   Why does making an error make me a jerk? It doesn't except in my own head. I believe that doing something wrong makes me stupid or a jerk. Nothing I can do can make me anything. I am not my behavior. As long as I live I will make mistakes, so I better get used to it and stop exaggerating the importance and insisting I don't make any. Instead of blaming myself, it would be far better for me to use all my energy towards correcting my mistakes, where possible.

Discuss with your teacher and classmates what else you want to add in answering the WHY questions above.

GA1139

# Review

Let's review how you can take responsibility for feeling good.

A. Something unpleasant happens.

B. You evaluate with your attitudes and beliefs.

C. You get upset.

D. You question.

E. You answer accurately.

Take responsibility for your feelings in the situation below. Write out each step and think it through.

A. Your brother or sister or friend borrows something of yours without asking.

B. Beliefs or attitudes

_____

_____

_____

_____

C. Feelings (caused by your beliefs and attitudes)

_____

_____

_____

_____

D. Question (Ask WHY to your beliefs and attitudes.)

_____

_____

_____

_____

E. Answer (Answer your WHYS logically and sensibly.)

_____

_____

_____

_____

# Chapter 2
# Become Aware of Your Beliefs and Feelings

14

# Word Puzzle

Unscramble the following words and look up their meanings in your dictionary. You will find each of these words in this chapter.

alnoitra _____

Definition _____

nfoicnceed _____

Definition _____

ssrowlhte _____

Definition _____

citmaouat _____

Definition _____

eblaanosre _____

Definition _____

sseetnlia _____

Definition _____

uurrnntgi _____

Definition _____

cihpotrastac _____

Definition _____

rrocsenopgnid _____

Definition _____

queensce _____

Definition _____

lanoitarri _____

Definition _____

## Words

irrational
catastrophic
rational
sequence
confidence
worthless

automatic
nurturing
essential
reasonable
corresponding

GA1139

# Flunking Successfully

Write down the first five thoughts that you would say to yourself if you flunked an important exam.

_____
_____
_____
_____
_____
_____

Now imagine your best friend in tears because she flunked an important exam. Write the thoughts that you would say to her.

_____
_____
_____
_____
_____
_____

Compare the thoughts above. To whom were you kinder? Which thoughts will lead to a more positive emotional reaction? Which thoughts are more realistic, rational, sensible? Which thoughts are punishing and hurtful? Would you ever treat yourself like you treat a friend? Would you ever treat a friend like you treat yourself? Why or why not?

Which thoughts will help build a good self-image? Which thoughts will help to build confidence for the next test?

GA1139

# Weeding Your Garden

You wanted Dad to allow you to care for the garden in your backyard. Instead he gives the job to your older brother. You feel rejected and worthless.

Color the weeds in the garden below which have beliefs written on them about the event above that causes you to feel rejected and worthless.

Color the weeds green which have accurate beliefs written on them about the event above that would cause you to feel confident and worthwhile.

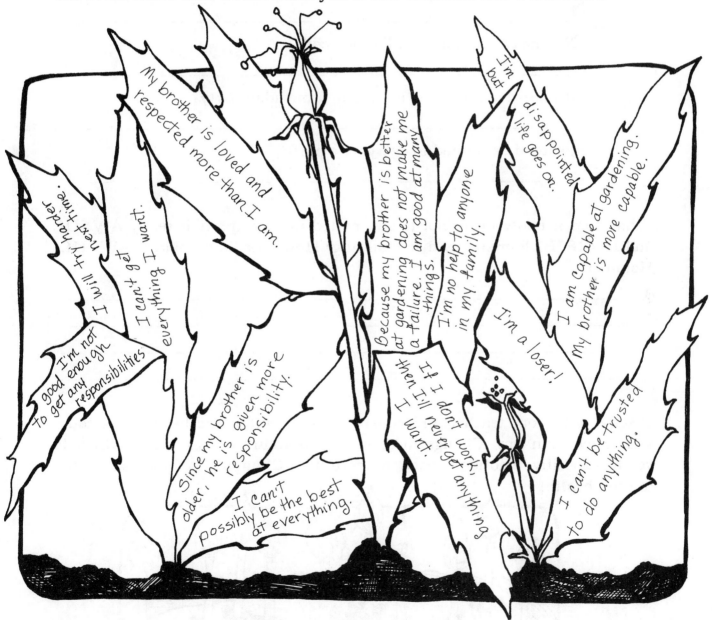

NOTICE that it is the way you choose to think about a situation which causes your emotional reaction, not the situation itself. You always have a choice as to how you feel!

17

# Changing Your Tapes

Situation: Sally does not get invited to a classmate's birthday party.

Push the ON button of the tape recorder and listen to the automatic beliefs that go on in Sally's mind. How do you think these beliefs make Sally feel?

In order for Sally to feel better about herself, she needs to change her tape. It's old and worn out. Help her rewrite her tape by changing her unreasonable thoughts to reasonable ones.

A. **ON**  I'm the most unpopular kid in the whole school.

_____

No one cares about me. I'm no good.

_____

It's horrible not to get invited to a birthday party.

_____

I should be invited to everyone's party.

_____

What does it really mean not to get invited to a party? Is it really AWFUL and HORRIBLE or simply disappointing? How does Sally make it AWFUL? Help her!

B. _____

_____

_____

_____

Discuss with your teacher and classmates your automatic beliefs that cause you to feel unhappy. Change these beliefs to accurate ones which will help you have positive emotional reactions more often. Changing old tapes is essential to good health!

GA1139

# Seeds That Will Help You Grow

Situation: You do not get chosen for the tennis team.

Cut out the seeds below which have written on them beliefs or thoughts about the event above that would help you remain confident about yourself. Paste each seed in the bottom of a flowerpot and draw a flower blooming and growing from this seed. Watch yourself bloom and grow as you plant these nurturing thoughts about yourself in your head and heart.

GA1139

# Lost in the Woods

Situation: You are taking a walk in the woods. You get lost. You don't know which way to turn. You notice footsteps on the ground. Follow the footsteps that you believe will lead you in the right direction. Color the footsteps brown as you step in them. Avoid the footsteps which will keep you trapped. See if you can get out of the woods. Good luck!

Discuss with your teacher and classmates why you chose your footsteps. What about the beliefs written in them that helped lead you in the right direction? How would the other beliefs keep you trapped?

20

# Mix and Match

Draw and color each sequence of events in the corresponding box below. Then cut out and shuffle the boxes and ask classmates, friends and family to try to arrange them in the correct sequence. Remember to cut out ONLY the boxes—leave off the numbers.

| 1 | 2 | 3 | 4 | 5 | 6 | 7 |
|---|---|---|---|---|---|---|
|   |   |   |   |   |   |   |

1. Your friend comes in last in the two-mile foot race.

2. He tells himself that he's a loser, a wimp, lazy, clumsy, and will never succeed at anything.

3. He leans against a pole and cries.

4. You put your arm around him and tell him all the reasons why calling himself a wimp, loser, failure, etc., for losing a race are irrational thoughts.

5. Tell him why losing a race may be disappointing but not AWFUL, HORRIBLE, CATASTROPHIC—and why it is nice to win a race, but there is no law saying one MUST or SHOULD always win.

6. A light bulb goes off in your friend's head as you speak. He begins to smile and feel relieved.

7. He walks away telling you more realistic beliefs about himself—"I can't be the best at everything I try, but I'm happy to have the courage to try."

Discuss with your classmates, friends and family why he was able to change from feeling upset to feeling relief.

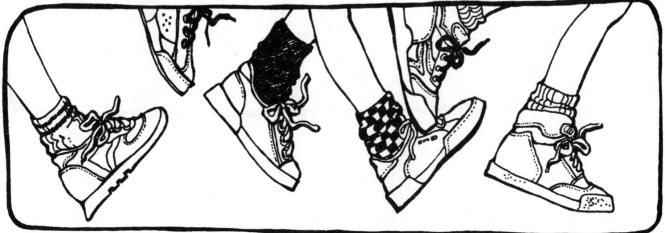

GA1139

# Chapter 3
# Thinking Responsibly

GA1139

# Word Puzzle

See how many of the vocabulary words below you can find in the chapter. Underline the word in green when you find it on a page and circle it in black when you know its definition.

frustration _____

disappointment_____

actually_____

magnify _____

catastrophe_____

relatively _____

scenario _____

self-esteem _____

self-confidence _____

personalizing _____

communicate _____

guilt _____

shame_____

imperfect _____

irresponsible_____

unreasonable _____

partially _____

absolutely _____

conclusions _____

rational_____

irrational _____

dispute _____

GA1139

# Should Madness

Write the ways in which you believe things SHOULD be about each category below.

My friends SHOULD always:
(for example) call me every day.

_____

_____

_____

My friends ACTUALLY:
(for example) call me once a week.

_____

_____

_____

I SHOULD always know:

_____

_____

_____

I ACTUALLY know:

_____

_____

_____

My teachers SHOULD never:

_____

_____

_____

My teachers actually never:

_____

_____

_____

My family SHOULD know:

_____

_____

_____

My family ACTUALLY knows:

_____

_____

_____

People in my neighborhood SHOULD never:

_____

_____

_____

People in my neighborhood ACTU-ALLY never:

_____

_____

_____

Put an X next to each of the statements above which does not usually happen the way you believe it SHOULD. Discuss with your teacher and classmates why things don't always happen as we believe they should and how thinking with strict SHOULDS and SHOULDN'TS can lead us to frustration, anger and disappointment.

Next to each X write the way that situation ACTUALLY happens.

How would you feel if you began to accept how things ACTUALLY are rather than how you believe they SHOULD be? What could you gain by thinking like this? What could you lose? Discuss together with your teacher and classmates. Which is a more responsible way of thinking? Why?

# Magnify

For each event listed below, magnify its importance by turning it into a catastrophe. Make each catastrophe worse than the next.

For example:

You fail an important test.

This is the end of the world for me.

I am going to be killed.

I'll probably never get into a college.

You don't make the tennis team.

_____

_____

_____

You miss your bus.

_____

_____

_____

Your dog gets sick.

_____

_____

_____

You lose your gloves.

_____

_____

_____

Read these aloud to your teacher and classmates. Have the other students add to your list of catastrophes—ones you hadn't even thought of. Disscuss how easy it is to make a relatively unimportant event into what feels like a life or death situation—a true catastrophe—just by the way we choose to think about the situation.

GA1139

# Getting Straight Our Magnifications

Now that you've created your worst possible thoughts about each situation, try writing the best that might happen and then write the most probable.

For example:

You fail an important test.

(Best) You get a tutor and get the help you need.

(Probable) You learn from your mistakes and improve the next time.

You don't make the tennis team.

(Best) _____

(Probable) _____

You miss your bus.

(Best) _____

(Probable) _____

Your dog gets sick.

(Best) _____

(Probable) _____

You lose your gloves.

(Best) _____

(Probable) _____

Discuss with your teacher and classmates the difference in your feelings when you think realistically about a situation rather than when you magnify and "catastrophize" a situation. Note which thoughts help you feel calmer and more confident. What would you gain by thinking more accurately? What would you lose? Which is a more responsible way of thinking? Why?

GA1139

# Label Me Accurately, Please!

Illustrate each scenario and then cut out one of the three titles below each which most ACCURATELY and REALISTICALLY describes the character in the scene. Paste that on as the title of the illustration.

1. Sally cannot get herself organized. Her alarm is ringing, she can't find her socks, she accidently knocks the books off her shelf and her cat is chewing on last night's homework.

**Paste Title Here**

---

## Choose a Title

| A Difficult Morning for Sally | Stupid Sally | Clumsy Sally |

2. Burt gets on skis for the first time and falls over. All the kids laugh. He finally picks himself up and down he goes again. This time his leg is in one direction and his arm in another and one of his skis is flying down the hill.

**Paste Title Here**

---

## Choose a Title

| Clutzy Burt | Burt Tries to Ski | Burt the Wimp |

Discuss with your teacher and classmates why labeling people (and/or yourself) with bad names like *wimp, clutz, stupid, clumsy* is inaccurate and not a responsible way of thinking about yourself, others and situations. Turn to the next activity to learn more about labeling.

GA1139

# More About Labeling

Now Burt thinks that he is a real clutz. Since he couldn't stand up on skis the first time, he labeled himself a clutz and told himself that he will never be able to ski or do any sports.

Help Burt feel better about himself, think more accurately and realistically about his abilities and take more responsibility for how he thinks by completing the ABCDE model introduced in Chapter 1.

A. Situation
Burt falls down on his skis his first time out.

B. His beliefs (about the situation)
Example: I'm a clutz.

_____

_____

_____

C. Feelings (caused by his beliefs)
Example: shame

_____

_____

_____

D. Dispute beliefs by asking why.
Example: Why does it mean you are a clutz if you fall down when learning to ski?

_____

_____

_____

E. Logically and sensibly answer the whys.
Example: It does not mean you are a clutz if you fall down. You cannot learn to ski like you can't learn to walk without falling. It is part of the process of learning.

_____

_____

_____

Labeling yourself or others can result in hurt and inaccurate feelings and low self-esteem. Before labeling yourself or others, use the model above to help yourself see yourself, others and situations accurately and responsibly.

Write the three most common words with which you label yourself. (For example: spoiled, lazy, wimp) _____    _____    _____

Now for each label, write three examples of how you are not those things.
(For example: I'm not lazy when I spent yesterday cleaning the basement.)

_____    _____    _____

_____    _____    _____

_____    _____    _____

Labels, as you can see, are inaccurate. We are all, at times, lazy or wimpy and at other times and in other situations strong and active. What do you gain from labeling yourself or others? What do you lose? Discuss with your teacher and classmates. Which is a more responsible way of thinking? Why?

GA1139

# Mountains out of Molehills

Did you ever hear the expression, "You are making a mountain out of a molehill"? John's fuzzy monster who lives within him does this all the time. Many things that happen to John, fuzzy monster makes a mountain of. Draw mountains around any statements that show fuzzy monster at work.

John does not make the tennis team. He tells himself that he will never make another team in his life.

John fails a test. He tells himself that he will have to study harder next time and perhaps get a tutor for some extra help.

John gets stood up by a girl he asked out. He tells himself that girls will never like or go out with him since Donna didn't want to.

John gets yelled at for coming home late. John realizes what caused him to be late and thinks of ways to prevent that from happening next time.

John buys the wrong items in the grocery store. He tells himself that he will never be able to follow directions.

Fuzzy monster creates mountains by exaggerating. He says if something happens one time it will happen every time. Is that true? Can you dispute this inaccurate belief? What is inaccurate about it? Discuss with your teacher and classmates how thinking like this can cause a person to lose confidence in himself. Discuss the situations in which John's fuzzy monster did not create a mountain allowing John to think sensibly and responsibly. How will he gain confidence by thinking responsibly?

GA1139

# Challenging Your Fuzzy Monster

Describe four situations in which your fuzzy monster made a mountain out of a molehill. For each situation, challenge your monster, so that you can think more accurately about the situation, take responsibility and increase your self-confidence.

Example:

Situation: I lost my wallet. I told myself I would never be able to handle money.

Challenge: It is not true that because I lose my wallet once or twice that I can never learn how to handle money. Instead and more accurately it means that when I carry money in my wallet, I will keep my wallet in my front pocket and check for it before I leave a store. This will reduce the chances of my leaving it on the counter.

GA1139

# It's All My Fault

Think of as many ways as you can to make each of the following events all your fault.

A classmate decides to switch classrooms because she wants to be with different kids.
It's my fault she's moving because (example) I wasn't friendly enough.

_____

_____

_____

_____

Your parents are getting a divorce.
It's my fault my parents are getting divorced because (example) I didn't do well in school and my parents fought over how to help me.

_____

_____

_____

_____

Your father is angry at your mother all the time.
It's my fault that my father is always angry with my mother because (example) I should be able to keep my father in a good mood.

_____

_____

_____

_____

Discuss with your teacher and classmates which of these events could really be your fault and for which you are not at all responsible. How do you know the difference? Do you take responsibility for things with your family and friends that are not at all YOUR responsibility and that you have no control over? Why? Do you take personally everything that happens around you? The next exercise will help you not make everything all your fault.

GA1139

# Maybe It Is Not All My Fault

Use the ABCDE model that you learned in Chapter 1 to help you know what you are responsible for in relationships and what you are not. Help yourself to stop personalizing everything!

A. Situation

Your parents get divorced.

B. Beliefs

Example: If I had done better in school, my parents would not have fought as much.

_____

C. Feelings

Example: guilt _____   _____   _____

D. Dispute beliefs.

Example: Why should my abilities in school have anything to do with my parents staying married?

_____

_____

_____

E. Logically and sensibly answer the whys.

Example: How I do in school should have nothing to do with my parents staying married. I am responsible to do the best I can in school, but it is my parents' decision if they choose to fight rather than communicate over their concerns about me. I am not responsible for how they decide to cope.

_____

_____

_____

You can see how easy it is to blame yourself for things you are not responsible for or have no control over. This behavior leads to feelings of guilt, shame and low self-esteem. Use the ABCDE model for other situations in which you blame yourself and see if you can learn to take responsibility by not taking responsibility for the things you are not responsible for. Learn to be responsible only for what you are responsible for and can have control over.

GA1139

# Be Perfectly Perfect

Write a perfect story below about a perfect girl or boy who has the perfect parents, friends and teachers, and write about that person's perfect day at a perfect school. Make sure your grammar and creativity are perfect.

_____

_____

_____

_____

_____

_____

_____

_____

_____

_____

_____

_____

_____

_____

Discuss with your perfect teacher and classmates what it felt like to try to be perfect. Is it possible to be perfect? Why or why not? What do you gain and what do you lose when you try to be perfect? Do you always try to be perfect? Why and for whom? What would be a more possible and more realistic way to be? Does trying to be perfect help develop your self-esteem or hinder its development? Why?

On the next page experiment with being imperfect.

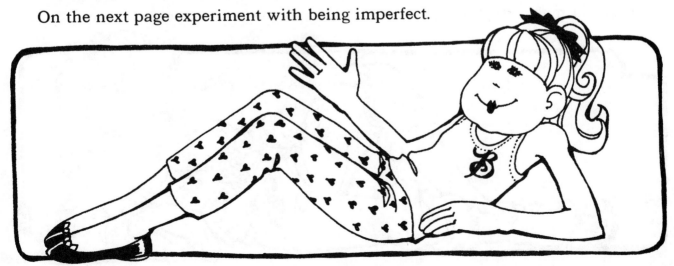

GA1139

# Permission to Be Imperfect

Write an imperfect story below about an imperfect boy and girl who have imperfect parents, friends and teachers. Write about their imperfect day at school. Make sure your grammar and creativity are imperfect.

_____
_____
_____
_____
_____
_____
_____
_____
_____
_____
_____
_____
_____
_____

Discuss with your imperfect teacher and classmates what it felt like to be imperfect. How is it different from trying to be perfect? Which creates less pressure on you and helps you to think straighter? Which is more realistic—to be perfect or imperfect?

Remember it is important to always strive to be the best you can, but it is impossible for anyone to ever be perfect. So in order to be the best you can, you must accept and give yourself permission to be imperfect.

34

GA1139

# Red or Yellow?

Read the following statements and then write each one in either the red or yellow column.

You do not get asked to dance once at the party. You must be unattractive.

You get the highest grade on your math test. You must be the smartest kid ever.

You get yelled at by your gym teacher. You must be a real loser.

You write an essay that won awards. You are the greatest essay writer.

No one called you for dates this weekend. Your friends must not like you anymore.

You are told by two people that they don't like your dress. You must have no taste in clothes.

You forget your lunch on the way to school—first time ever. You must be irresponsible and forgetful.

Write each statement under the column you think it fits under. Red shows that you are a loser and yellow statements show that you are a winner.

| Red | Yellow |
| --- | --- |
|  |  |
|  |  |
|  |  |
|  |  |
|  |  |

Discuss with your teacher and classmates what is irrational and unreasonable about the kind of thinking above? Can anyone be a total loser or total winner? Why or why not? If something negative happens to you, does that incident make you a total winner or loser? Why or why not? What is irresponsible about this kind of thinking? Does it enhance self-esteem?

The next exercise will help you understand and recognize the shades between the reds and yellows.

GA1139

# Shades of Orange

Do the following exercises and write your answers in the blank spaces.

Look at your desk. Is it perfectly neat? Is every inch piled with a heap of junk? Or is it partially neat? _____

Look at yourself in the mirror. Are you completely satisfied with everything you see or are there some things you are satisfied with and other parts of yourself you are not? List what you are and are not satisfied with.

_____

Look at your classroom. Is it perfectly clean? Is every inch piled with dust and clutter or is it partially clean?_____

Look at your handwriting. Is it perfect penmanship? What do you like about it and what do you feel can be improved? _____

Look at the streets in your neighborhood. Are they perfectly clean? Is every inch piled with litter so that you can no longer see the street? Or are they partially clean?_____

There is no such thing as PERFECT anything. There is no such thing that is ABSOLUTELY one way or ABSOLUTELY another. Everything in the world has shades. The more you are able to see the shades in situations the better you will feel about yourself and the world. Otherwise you will see yourself and others in one of two ways only—total loser or total winner. You measure up or you don't. Shades help you to see yourself and others more realistically.

Write the ways in which you see yourself a total winner, a total loser and somewhere in between.

| Red—Total Loser | Orange—In-Between | Yellow—Total Winner |
| --- | --- | --- |
|  |  |  |

# Absolutely!

Copy from the previous exercise your total loser and total winner statements below. Look at each statement carefully and find your irrational and unreasonable ways of thinking, causing you to feel RESOLUTELY one way or the other. Challenge each, using the ABCDE model and find your shades of gray.

**Total Loser Statements**          **Irrational Ideas**          **Shades of Gray**

**Total Winner Statements**

Discuss with your teacher and classmates how it feels not to think of yourself and others as totally winners or totally losers. What does it do for your self-confidence? Do you feel more responsible to yourself and others? Why or why not?

GA1139

# Red, Orange and Yellow Mosaic

Color each piece of the mosaic either red, orange or yellow by following the key below.

Red:      all statements showing ABSOLUTE thinking causing the person to feel like a loser

Orange:  all statements not showing ABSOLUTE thinking

Yellow:  all statements showing ABSOLUTE thinking causing the person to feel like a total winner

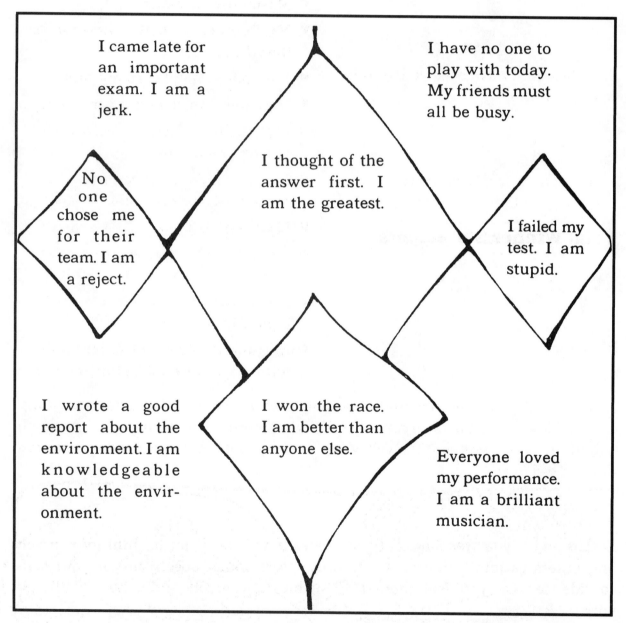

I came late for an important exam. I am a jerk.

I have no one to play with today. My friends must all be busy.

No one chose me for their team. I am a reject.

I thought of the answer first. I am the greatest.

I failed my test. I am stupid.

I wrote a good report about the environment. I am knowledgeable about the environment.

I won the race. I am better than anyone else.

Everyone loved my performance. I am a brilliant musician.

Cut and hang your mosaic.

GA1139

# Jumping to Conclusions

What are the conclusions you might jump to when the following situations take place? Draw a line from the situation to your probable conclusion.

A friend does not return your call.

A teacher never calls on you for answers.

Your father always asks your brother to help him.

Your mother has little time for you and your problems.

- My father likes my brother better.
- My friend does not like me anymore. I must not be likeable.
- My teacher has given up on me because I'm stupid.
- My mother is busy.
- My brother is better at repairs than I am.
- I am not as helpful as my brother.
- My friend is sick of me. I'm a pain.
- My teacher doesn't realize she doesn't call on me.
- I am a failure since my father doesn't ask for my help.
- My friend is busy.
- I am stupid because my teacher does not call on me.
- My mother dislikes me. I must be a pain in the neck.
- My mother does not enjoy being with me. I must not be fun enough.

Discuss with your teacher and classmates the kinds of conclusions you jump to. Are they rational or irrational? Why? Are the conclusions you jump to helpful to your self-confidence? Why or why not? Are the conclusions you jump to accurate?

GA1139

# Possible Conclusions

Why doesn't anyone call you? Why are you not called on?

List below under each situation ALL the possible conclusions you can come to. Then brainstorm a list and have your teacher write them all on the board. The next activity will help you learn ways to find out the most accurate conclusion.

A friend does not return your call.

ALL POSSIBLE CONCLUSIONS

_____

_____

_____

_____

Your teacher never calls on you for answers.

ALL POSSIBLE CONCLUSIONS

_____

_____

_____

_____

Your father always asks your brother to help him, never you.

ALL POSSIBLE CONCLUSIONS

_____

_____

_____

_____

Your mother has little time to spend with you.

ALL POSSIBLE CONCLUSIONS

_____

_____

_____

_____

GA1139

# Accurate Conclusions

What are the ways you can prevent yourself from jumping to the wrong conclusions about situations and events that happen to you and jump to the accurate conclusion instead? Circle below those ways that would seem helpful to determining the correct conclusion.

A friend does not return your call. I could:

Ask my friend why she didn't return my call.

Assume the worst and not ask.

Imagine my worst beliefs about myself and imagine that that is what my friend is thinking.

Think negative thoughts about myself like, "Why would anyone want to talk to me anyway?"

Think accurate thoughts about myself like, "There doesn't seem to be any reason I can think of that my friend wouldn't call me back. I had better check with him/her and find out his/her reason and if everything is OK."

Think carefully about my recent behavior with my friend and try to recognize if there's something I might have done or said that pushed him/her away. If not, I had better check and see if he/she is OK.

Just never call him/her back again and stay angry.

Talk to him/her about my feelings when he/she doesn't return calls.

Figure he/she is not a good friend after all and not bother.

Discuss with your teacher and classmates other possibilities that would be helpful in determining the correct conclusion. Discuss the answers you have circled—discuss whether those would be the helpful ones. Why and why not?

GA1139

# Wrong Conclusion

Write a story about a time you jumped to the wrong conclusion about a situation. Describe what happened as a result of jumping to the wrong conclusion. What would you do differently or how would you think differently next time? Read your story to your classmates.

42

# Right Conclusion

Now write the same story as in the previous exercise, but this time jump to the accurate conclusion. Write a new ending based on the more accurate conclusion. Read your story to your classmates.

43

# Kinds of Irrational Thinking

We have discussed in this chapter the different kinds of irrational thinking that cause us not to feel good about ourselves or others. Review the kinds of irrational thinking discussed. Do you understand why they are irrational?

Shoulds and Shouldn'ts—You try to push yourself by saying I SHOULD or I SHOULDN'T. Although there are many things you should and shouldn't do, too much of this kind of thinking will cause you to feel pressured and resentful. When you put too many SHOULDS and SHOULDN'TS on others, you are insisting on perfection and will end up frustrated and angry. You want to try to think about the way things actually are rather than the way you think they SHOULD be.

Magnifying and "Catastrophizing"—You exaggerate the importance of things and make it into a catastrophe. You blow things out of proportion. Many things are very important and serious; however, when you blow it out of size the situation can cause you to become unnecessarily nervous or upset.

Labeling—Instead of simply identifying your mistake, you add a judgement onto yourself like, I am a loser, or to someone else's error, he is a jerk.

Overgeneralizing—You make yourself believe that if one thing happens it will happen over and over again to you. If you fail one test, you will fail them all. If one person does not like you, that means no one will ever like you.

Personalizing—You see yourself as the cause of everything. Although you are responsible for many things, you make yourself responsible for things that you really have no control over. A classmate moves away. You think that if you were a better friend to her she wouldn't move.

All or Nothing (Black or White)—If you are not perfect, you see yourself or others as total losers. You do not see the shades of gray. You demand perfection.

Jumping to Conclusions—You make negative conclusions even though you have nothing to support those conclusions.

Use these definitions to help you with the next exercise.

44

GA1139

# Identifying Irrational Ways of Thinking

See if you can identify the kinds of irrational thinking in each of the statements below. Use the definitions on the previous page.

## Choices

Shoulds/Shouldn'ts
Magnifying/"Catastrophizing"
Labeling
Overgeneralizing
Personalizing
Black or White

| Statements | Identification |
|---|---|
| I'm a real wimp. I can't even fix my bike! | |
| I'll never be able to learn this. I got a 50 on my last test. | |
| Isn't it horrible that Sally did not get asked to the dance? | |
| I should be better at the parallel bars by now. | |
| If I did a better job in school, maybe my parents would love me more. | |
| Since I am the only one who learned how to swim, I must be the most athletic. | |

# Chapter 4
# Developing
# Responsible
# Attitudes

## Getting Rid of SHOULDS and HORRIBLES

# Word Puzzle

Find the vocabulary words hidden in the word maze, circle them and write their definitions below. Enjoy!

```
D I S A S T E R S T M E C K R S O M E S A
I I M C K R U N D O V R K U G H O M N U R
S L C D V C M D C E C H E K L V A B D E M
P U W X C T A E O V L O U E N K R C T B E
E R E T S M O U C L D R M E U G H A B R C
U N F O R T U N A T E X P E R I E N C E D
T A U Z O M E B C M N B E I D L B A R L S
E N E V A R E R C O Y A R D R L D W A K E
M A B L I L U Q U V G J N E T U J R R Y M
D I S P U T E L R R I N D A S S Y Q U E S
T W D D Y O C B A L D R U L E T F L D N T
G S L U Q W I D D U N O C O M R M N U I F
C A T E E N A G E N M T N E U A R S T L D
C A T S T P E H N O E L P E O T N U R X G
D E N I G E R A Y P T E S T H E V W X I S
```

## Words to Find

disasters        _____

unfortunate      _____

experienced      _____

dispute          _____

deny             _____

illustrate       _____

GA1139

# I Must Always Be Liked

Valerie was very upset. She heard through the grapevine that one of her classmates did not like her. She cried and cried when she got home. She told her mother that she didn't think she could survive knowing that someone did not like her. She decided she no longer liked herself and could not face the other kids at school. Maybe they secretly didn't like her either.

Why do you think Valerie believed that she had to be liked by everyone? Do you believe this?

_____

_____

How did she make herself feel about herself if others did not like her?

_____

_____

Is it true that if someone does not like Valerie then that must mean that she is not OK? What does it *actually* mean?

_____

_____

Is it REALLY possible to be liked by EVERYONE? Why or why not? What is more probable?

_____

_____

Is Valerie responsible to make EVERYONE like her? What is her responsibility to others?

_____

_____

Help Valerie to dispute her belief that she MUST be liked by EVERYONE in order for her to like herself by using the ABCDE model on the next page. Help her to replace her old belief with a new and more realistic belief.

GA1139

# Changing Valerie's Irrational Belief

A. Situation
   Valerie hears through the grapevine that someone does not like
   her.

D. Dispute beliefs.
   _____
   _____
   _____

E. Sensibly answer the why.
   _____
   _____
   _____
   _____
   _____

B. Beliefs
   _____
   _____
   _____

C. Feelings
   _____
   _____
   _____

How do you think Valerie will feel about herself if she has a more sensible and responsible belief? Do you see how simply changing a belief to be more realistic can change the way you feel about yourself and others?

49

GA1139

# That's More Horrible Than Horrible

Fill in the blanks below to complete the sentences.

1. It's horrible when _____

2. The most horrible thing that has ever happened to me was _____
   _____

3. The most horrible thing that could happen to me would be _____
   _____

4. The most horrible thing that I've ever seen was_____
   _____

5. The most horrible thing that I've ever heard was_____
   _____

The attitude behind HORRIBLE is almost always an unrealistic exaggeration. This kind of thinking turns unfortunate situations into disasters.

Try to challenge your HORRIBLES by asking, why is it horrible? Where is my proof? When you examine situations carefully, you will notice that nothing is HORRIBLE. The situation may be unpleasant or unfortunate or terribly sad or disappointing, but it is only your "disastrous" thinking that causes it to be HORRIBLE.

Below write more realistic and accurate accounts of the "horrible" situations written about above.

1. _____

2. _____

3. _____

4. _____

5. _____

GA1139

# Horrible/Awful Story

Write your own story using lots of shoulds, horribles and awfuls. In other words, write a story with lots of exaggerations, making unpleasant situations into disastrous ones. Ask a classmate to read your story and to circle in red all the unrealistic exaggerations he/she can find.

_____

_____

_____

_____

_____

_____

_____

_____

_____

_____

_____

_____

GA1139

# Learning How to Accept Yourself

Write something you've done that you are not proud of and don't like to admit about yourself.

_____

_____

Just writing it should help you accept rather than deny that this was your behavior.

Unless you are willing to admit to your behaviors, you will not be able to change what you do not like. If you do not admit that you have a hurt arm, you cannot fix it.

Now try to understand yourself rather than beat yourself up. Write down those things that caused you to do what you did.
Example: I did not return my sister's sweater because she didn't let me play with her friends.

Try to understand your feelings at the time which caused you to act irrationally.
Example: I was feeling hurt and rejected so I wanted to hurt her back.

Now try to understand why you did what you did without necessarily accepting or liking your behavior.

Once you understand yourself and your reaction, decide how you would prefer to react next time. What would be more rational and more responsible?

_____

_____

_____

_____

Discuss with your teacher and classmates why you must first admit to your behaviors before changing them.

GA1139

# Guess the Missing Thoughts

Box 1 names the event. Box 3 names the feelings the person involved in the event experienced.

Write in Box 2 the thoughts or beliefs the person probably had about the event causing her to feel the feelings named in Box 3. Illustrate each box.

| **Box 1**<br>Jane gets the flu and can't go on the class trip. | **Box 2** | **Box 3**<br>Jane feels very angry. |
|---|---|---|
| **Box 1**<br>Laura does not get asked to the dance. | **Box 2** | **Box 3**<br>Laura feels like a loser and reject. |

The exercise on the next page will ask you to help Jane and Laura to think more accurately and responsibly so their self-esteem can improve.

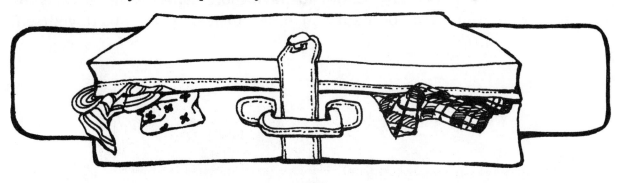

GA1139

# Changing the Missing Thoughts

Box 1 names the same event. Box 3 names different feelings than listed in the last exercise that the person involved in the event experienced. Write the thoughts or beliefs the person probably had about the event causing her to feel the feelings named. Illustrate each box.

| Box 1 | Box 2 | Box 3 |
|---|---|---|
| Jane gets the flu and can't go on the class trip. | | Jane feels sad, but optimistic and loved. |
| **Box 1**<br>Laura does not get asked to the dance. | **Box 2** | **Box 3**<br>Laura feels disappointed. |

Discuss with your teacher and classmates why changing thoughts can change how a person feels. Why is it more responsible to think more accurately? How will this help Jane and Laura to have more self-esteem? What ways of thinking do you need to change in order to feel better about yourself?

GA1139

# Chapter 5
# Developing
# Responsible
# Feelings

# Word Puzzle

Write the definitions of the following words found in this chapter by looking them up in your dictionary. Then take each word and see how many smaller words you can find in it (three or more letters). Have fun!

## irresponsible
Definition _____

Smaller words _____

_____

_____

## inferior
Definition _____

Smaller words _____

_____

_____

## compassionate
Definition _____

Smaller words _____

_____

_____

## corresponding
Definition _____

Smaller words _____

_____

GA1139

# Taking Responsibility for What You Feel

Answer the following questions as honestly as possible.

Write a situation in which you felt GUILTY.

_____

_____

_____

How did you make yourself feel guilty?

Example: I told myself I should never get angry at a friend.

_____

_____

_____

Write a situation in which you felt very ANGRY.

_____

_____

_____

How did you make yourself feel so angry?

_____

_____

_____

Write a situation in which you felt EMBARRASSED.

_____

_____

_____

How did you make yourself feel embarrassed?

_____

_____

_____

GA1139

# Feeling Responsibly

Try to figure out what caused each person to feel the way he/she feels.

1. Sally yells at Laura for being late to her party. Laura feels like a bad and irresponsible friend.

   What caused Laura to feel the way she does? _____

   _____

2. Peter drops his tray in the cafeteria. Everyone starts laughing and applauding. Peter turns bright red and runs out of the room embarrassed.

   What caused Peter to feel the way he does?_____

   _____

3. Carol received a lower grade on her project than her best friend Anne. Carol felt stupid and inferior.

   What caused Carol to feel the way she does? _____

   _____

Discuss with your teacher and classmates what actually causes people to feel the way they do. Is it the situation they are in or is it how they choose to think about the situation they are in? Discuss the ways in which you can take responsibility for how you feel?

The next exercise will help you to understand how each of the people above came to feel the way he/she does.

GA1139

# Taking a Closer Look

First, illustrate each box. Then write in the middle box all the thoughts that the person was probably thinking to cause his/her feelings. Remember the situation does NOT cause the person's feelings. It is HOW the person thinks about the situation.

Example: Carol did not end up feeling stupid and inferior because of her lower grade on a project. She felt stupid and inferior because she compared herself to her friend, because she told herself if someone else does better than she does, that means she is less of a person. These are irrational thoughts that cause her to put herself down unnecessarily.

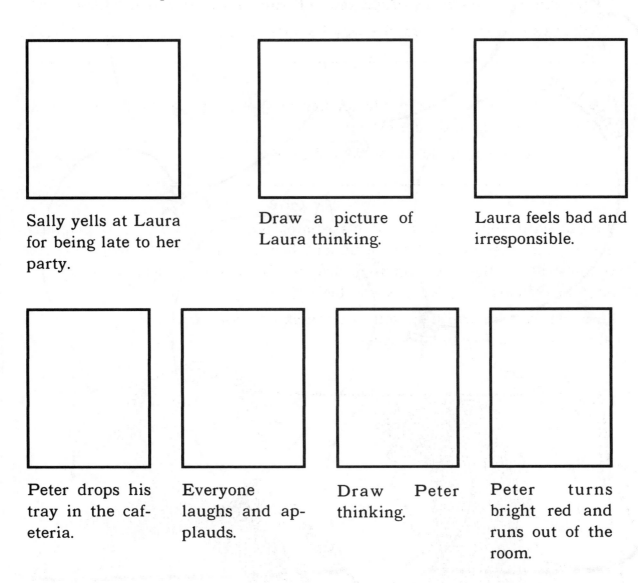

Sally yells at Laura for being late to her party.

Draw a picture of Laura thinking.

Laura feels bad and irresponsible.

Peter drops his tray in the cafeteria.

Everyone laughs and applauds.

Draw Peter thinking.

Peter turns bright red and runs out of the room.

Discuss with your teacher and classmates Peter's and Laura's inaccurate thinking about the situations. Suggest more accurate ways to think about the situations that would help them end up feeling better about themselves and more responsible for their feelings.

GA1139

# Flying High

Think of all the ways you help yourself to be happy. Write them in the balloons below.

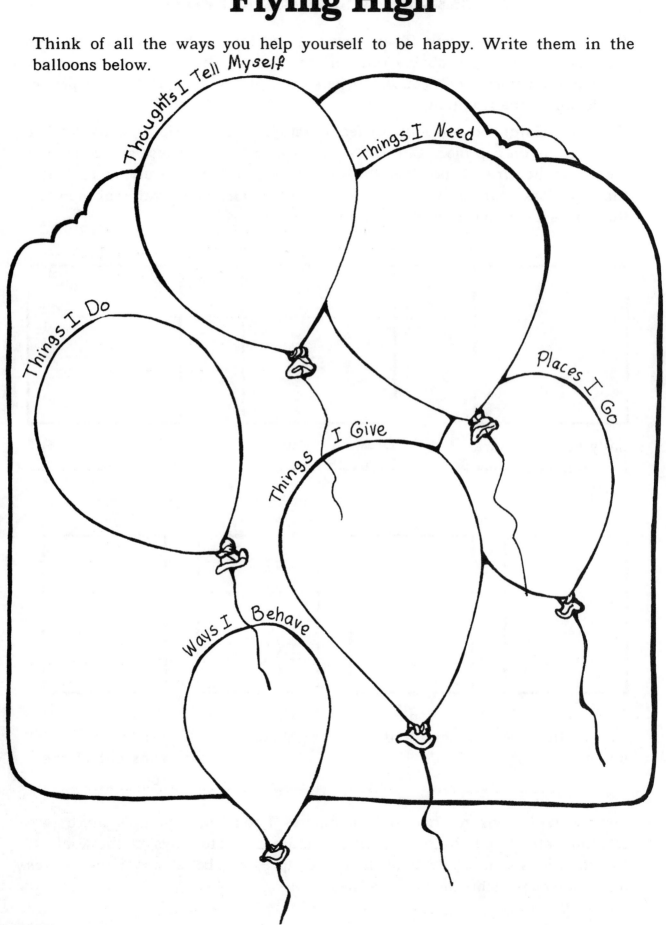

Thoughts I Tell Myself

Things I Need

Things I Do

Places I Go

Things I Give

Ways I Behave

60

GA1139

# Pen Pals

Write a letter to yourself. Tell yourself about a situation in your life right now that is causing you to feel anger or sadness or hurt or disappointment or guilt.

Dear _____,

_____

_____

_____

_____

_____

_____

_____

_____

_____

_____

_____

_____

_____

_____

_____

Love,

_____

Discuss with your teacher and classmates how to be compassionate with yourself. How do you know when you are treating yourself with respect? With no respect?

Tear this page out and send it to yourself at home. When you receive and read it, then go on to the next activity called CORRESPONDING. Answer your letter in the next activity.

GA1139

# Corresponding

Once you have received the letter you wrote to yourself in the mail, you are ready to write back. See how you feel when you read the letter. Do you feel sad or happy or scared for yourself? Write back with compassion and understanding in your response. Explain to yourself in the letter ways to think more rationally so that you can help yourself feel better.

Dear _____,

_____

_____

_____

_____

_____

_____

_____

_____

_____

_____

_____

_____

_____

_____

Love,

_____

Read your letter and response aloud and share them with your classmates. Then become pen pals with each other and help each other to think rationally. Thinking rationally and responsibly will help everyone feel better.

Remember to mail this letter to yourself.

GA1139

# Chapter 6
# Gaining Approval
# the Responsible
# Way

GA1139

# Word Puzzle

Try to guess what the italicized vocabulary words mean by using context clues. Then look up each word and write the dictionary definition. See how close you come.

You have done a great job. I know I can *depend* on you.

Guess _____

Dictionary definition _____


I feel proud when I win my mother's *approval.*

Guess _____

Dictionary definition _____


Zachary and Alex got the same *compliments* from their parents.

Guess _____

Dictionary definition _____


I got a good *evaluation* for the work I had accomplished.

Guess _____

Dictionary definition _____


The ticket is a *valid* one since it got me into the show.

Guess _____

Dictionary definition _____


I am *knowledgeable* about science since I have done research.

Guess _____

Dictionary definition _____

GA1139

# What's It Worth to You?

How much money would you give to get the following statements of approval from the following people? Write the amounts in the boxes.

| $5.00 | $25.00 | $50.00 | $100.00 |
|-------|--------|--------|---------|
| (least) | | | (most) |

## Person Giving Approval

| Statements of Approval | Parents | Siblings | Friends | Teacher | Self |
|---|---|---|---|---|---|
| You are very special to me. | | | | | |
| You are so creative! | | | | | |
| You have done a great job. I know I can depend on you. | | | | | |
| You look great! | | | | | |

Discuss with your teacher and classmates who you most want approval from and your reasons. Also notice the various kinds of approval you look for from the different people.

GA1139

# Winning Value

The way I try to win my mother's approval is _____
_____

The way I try to win my father's approval is _____
_____

The way I try to win my sister or brother's approval is _____
_____

The way I try to win my friends' approval is _____
_____

The way I try to win my teacher's approval is _____
_____

When I get any of these people's approval I feel _____
about myself.

When I do not get these people's approval I feel _____
about myself.

The person's approval that I try the hardest for is _____

The person I find it hardest to get approval from is _____

Discuss with your teacher and classmates what it means for you to get others' approval. Does it mean that you are a worthwhile person if you get their OK? Does it mean you are a good person? Or does it simply mean that your behavior in that particular situation was approved? Can someone else's approval of you make you valuable or lack of his approval make you not valuable? Explain.

GA1139

# Approving of Myself by Myself

Write in each heart a way in which you try to win your own approval.

Discuss with your teacher and classmates the difference between winning your own approval and winning others' approval of yourself. Does it feel different to you? How? Which do you trust more? Why? Which is more important? Why?

GA1139

# How Come?

Zachary and Alex got the same compliment from their parents. "I'm proud of you boys. You put a great deal of effort into fixing the car."

Zachary was thrilled to hear these words. He was feeling proud of himself. Alex, on the other hand, was not affected by these words. He did not feel proud of himself.

Why do you think Zachary ended up feeling good getting this approval and Alex did not? Remember they both did the same amount of work and got the same approval from their parents.

_____

_____

_____

_____

Discuss your answer with your teacher and classmates.

Do you have to agree or disagree with a compliment given to you to make it valid or invalid?

GA1139

# Buying Compliments

List situations in which compliments and approval from mother did not make you feel better about yourself. Discuss with your teacher and classmates the reasons.

_____

_____

_____

_____

List situations in which compliments and approval from father did not make you feel better about yourself. Discuss with your teacher and classmates the reason.

_____

_____

_____

_____

List situations in which compliments and approval from your teacher did not make you feel better about yourself. Discuss with your teacher and classmates the reason.

_____

_____

_____

_____

Is it possible that others' approval of you cannot REALLY affect your feelings about yourself? It is ONLY your own thoughts and beliefs that can ACTUALLY change your self-opinion. Someone else's approval has the ability to affect your self-opinion ONLY if YOU believe what he or she says is valid. In the previous exercise, Zachary believed that his parents' opinion of his performance was true so he felt good about himself. Alex did not believe what his parents said was valid so the approval did not make him feel better about himself. Alex did not think he did a good job on the car according to his own evaluation of himself; therefore he did not buy his parents' evaluation.

 GA1139

# Red or Blue?

Write in the circles the words of approval you would most like to hear about yourself from your mother, father, brothers, sisters, friends and teachers.

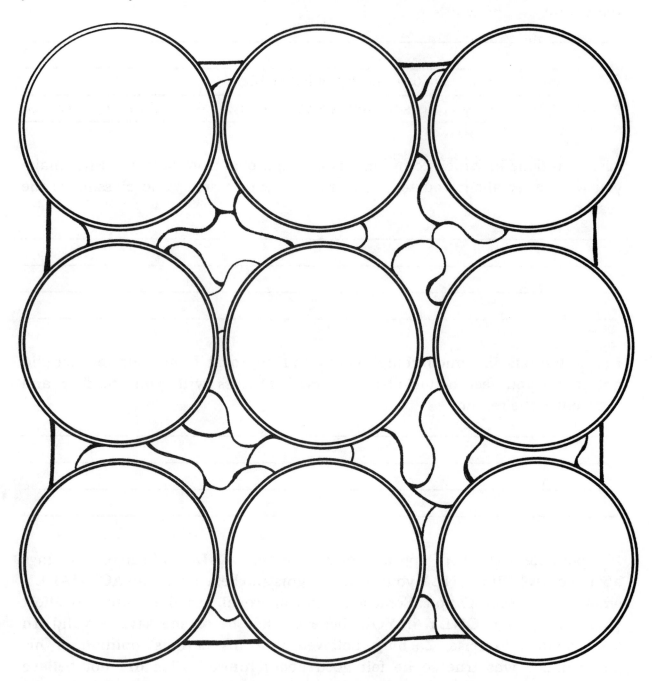

Color in red those which you believe about yourself and buy as valid. Color blue those you do not believe about yourself and do not buy as valid.

So whose approval really makes the difference in your feelings about yourself? Others' or your own? Why? Discuss with your teacher and classmates.

70

GA1139

# Cut and Paste

Cut out the blue circles from the exercise entitled Red or Blue. Paste them below. Under each write the ways in which you can help yourself to believe the validity of the words.

For example: You are smart.

- It is true that I am curious and knowledgeable.

- Although I am not the smartest person in my class, I think clearly and understand quickly.

- I do well enough on my tests.

GA1139

# Approval Seeking

Write the advantages and disadvantages of seeking approval from others.

| Advantages | Disadvantages |
|---|---|
|  |  |

Write the advantages and disadvantages of seeking approval from yourself.

| Advantages | Disadvantages |
|---|---|
|  |  |

What do you become aware of when you look over your lists of advantages and disadvantages? In which do you take more responsibility for yourself and your self-esteem? Why? How? Discuss with your teacher and classmates.

GA1139

# Behind Your Back

Write those things you approve of about yourself on the front of this person. Then on the back of this person (turn the page), write those things you do not approve of about yourself. Discuss with your teacher and classmates your reasons for disapproving and together use the ABCDE model to challenge the irrational beliefs that keep you from approving of yourself.

GA1139

# About-Face

Write those things you disapprove of in yourself and then fill in the ABCDE model. Are those things you disapprove of in others the same things you disapprove of in yourself? Discuss.

**A—Statement**

**B—Beliefs/Thoughts**

**C—Emotional Reaction**

**D—Dispute**

**E—Answer**

GA1139

# Chapter 7
# Handling
# Criticisms
# Responsibly

# Word Puzzles

Find ten words that you do not know the meanings of in this chapter. Write the words below and find their definitions in your dictionary. Then find ten words you already know the meanings of. Write their meanings below.

## New Vocabulary Words

_____     _____

_____     _____

_____     _____

_____     _____

_____     _____

_____     _____

_____     _____

_____     _____

## Words I Already Know

_____     _____

_____     _____

_____     _____

_____     _____

_____     _____

_____     _____

_____     _____

_____     _____

_____     _____

GA1139

# Warfare

Read this script between Mark and Joshua. What is the problem with the way Mark handles the criticism? Discuss with your teacher and classmates.

Joshua:     None of the kids like you. They all think you are mean and bossy.

Mark:        Well no one likes you either. Everyone thinks you are a wimp!

Joshua:     That's not true. Anyway, more kids don't like you than me!

Mark:        You can't even throw a baseball.

Joshua:     I can to. How would you know? You don't know anything.

Mark:        You want to bet? (Mark punches Joshua.)

Joshua:     (crying) I'm going to tell on you.

Mark:        You see you are a little wimp and a tattletale.

Mark defends, blames and attacks back, creating a war. Why does he do this?

Mark is obviously very afraid of criticism as most people are. That's because Mark thinks it's the other person's words that are hurtful rather than remembering it is actually his own self-criticism that is to fear. The only person in the world that has the power to put you down is YOU, but Mark forgot that in the face of criticism and felt he had to defend himself by attacking back.

Let's take a closer look at the automatic negative thoughts that went off in Mark's head.

Mark probably:

panicked—"This criticism shows that I really am worthless"—by jumping to conclusions.

exaggerates—Mark exaggerated the importance of what was said and assumed it definitely was true.

overgeneralized—"This means that I will be rejected by everyone always."

labeled—Mark automatically agreed with the criticism and labeled himself worthless. He didn't do this out loud but rather to himself. If he wasn't making such a harsh judgement on himself, he wouldn't have needed to defend so strongly. He simply would have let Joshua have his own opinion, but he wouldn't have bought it as valid.

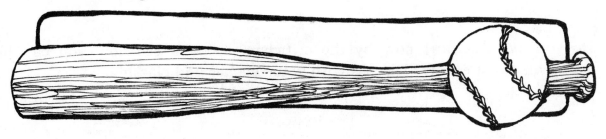

GA1139

# Ouch!

Write down a criticism that you have received that hurt your feelings. Then make a list of all your own negative thoughts that were triggered by this criticism. Take responsibility for your own hurt ouches by recognizing how you hurt yourself by your OWN self-criticism. Then next to each of your self-criticisms write down a rational response that is more reasonable and less hurtful.

For example:

## Automatic Negative Thought

(example using Mark from the Warfare exercise)

The kids found out the truth about me. I really am not likeable or popular and never will be.

## Rational Response

This is a silly idea. Just because someone says I'm mean and bossy doesn't mean I am a bad person. I can learn to change some undesirable behaviors, especially the ones that make others stay away from me.

## Criticism That I Have Received

_____

## My Automatic Negative Thoughts

_____
_____
_____
_____
_____

## More Rational Responses

_____
_____
_____
_____
_____

Do you feel less hurt now by the criticism? Do you see how you can be your own worst enemy? Discuss with your teacher and classmates.

# Question, Don't Attack

What would be a better way for Mark to handle the criticism? First, let's help Mark to remember some important information.

- If people criticize you, the information can either be RIGHT or WRONG.

- If the criticism is WRONG, you have nothing to be upset about. It's the other person's error, not yours, and you can't expect anyone to be perfect and never make errors, can you?

- If the criticism is RIGHT, you still don't have to be upset. You are not expected to be perfect, are you? Just acknowledge your error and do whatever you can to correct it.

So, if Mark will let himself be less than perfect, he can accept some of his faults and mistakes and maybe be more open to hearing them from others. Now when Mark is faced with criticism, he should try to ask questions (whether the critic is right or wrong) and avoid being judgmental or defensive. He should try to find out exactly what the person means by asking specific questions. Mark should try to see through the critic's eyes and find out exactly what it is that this person dislikes about him. This tactic will help get the critic off his back, the critic will feel listened to, the risk of being rejected completely is minimized and by seeing things the way the critic sees things the criticism, anger and hostility will be lessened. You will be working as a team to solve a problem rather than getting into warfare.

Joshua:    None of the kids like you. They all think you are mean and bossy.

Mark:      What do I do that makes the kids think of me as mean? As bossy?

Joshua:    Well, you tell them where to stand on the field and who can play and who can't.

Mark:      What exactly do the kids not like about my telling them where to stand?

Joshua:    Some kids have different ideas about how the game should be played and they don't feel they have a say.

Do you see how by Mark asking questions rather than defending he has helped the critic to be less angry, and now Mark has gathered some important information about the effects of his behavior on others? He can now think about ways he can change his behavior if he chooses.

GA1139

# Game 1
# Handling Criticism with Questions Only!

Play the Handling Criticism Game. Each of the exercises on the following pages has rules that you must follow while playing the game. Read the directions carefully.

Game 1:     Handling Criticism with Questions Only!

Directions:     You are to respond to the critic by asking him questions about his complaints ONLY! You are not allowed to be judgmental, defensive or attacking. Try to find out EXACTLY what this person dislikes about you, and try to see it through his/her eyes.

After you have written your script, read aloud with your teacher and classmates. Each classmate should make a red flag. He should hold up his red flag each time he hears you get defensive, attacking or judgmental or do anything other than ask questions about the complaint.

Critic: You are really stupid.

You: _____

Critic: I just think you are stupid. You act stupid and silly all the time.

You: _____

Critic: You are asking me so many questions. Why don't you just believe you are a stupid person!

You: _____
Critic: _____
You: _____
Critic: _____
You: _____
Critic: _____
You: _____
Critic: _____

Discuss with your teacher and classmates how many red flags you got and what self-criticisms you were making of yourself when you went back to defending, attacking or judging. How do you feel at the end of this dialogue if you didn't get any red flags?

# Agree, Don't Attack

Have you ever been criticized or attacked, yet you know the criticism is completely WRONG? You probably try to immediately defend yourself and tell the other person how wrong he is. Unfortunately, this probably creates warfare. Try a new tactic instead. Try to find something about what the person is saying to agree with—either just in principle or that you understand how upset the person is or find some grain of truth somehow. Here's an example using Joshua and Mark's dialogue.

| | |
|---|---|
| Joshua: | None of the kids like you. They all think you are mean and bossy. |
| Mark: | I know that I have at times been mean or bossy. |
| Joshua: | Well everyone hates you because of it. |
| Mark: | I know that being mean and bossy is not likeable and can understand why some people might hate me for it. I don't like to be disliked or hated and would like to be less mean and bossy. Maybe you could help me to see when I'm acting this way. |
| Joshua: | I don't want to help you. You have been mean to me. |
| Mark: | I understand that you have been hurt by my meanness. I will try my best to learn how to be less mean and bossy. |

How about when you have been criticized and attacked and you know the criticism is pretty accurate? Again, try to agree with the critic so you lessen his/her anger. He feels listened to, and you stay open to hearing what might be helpful feedback for you (as long as you remind yourself it is OK not to be perfect and know everything).

| | |
|---|---|
| Critic: | You were really rude to me on the telephone yesterday. |
| You: | You are absolutely right. I was rushed and rude. |
| Critic: | I didn't like it. You made me angry, and I never want to speak to you again. |
| You: | I'm sorry for my behavior yesterday. I want you to know that I did not mean or want to hurt your feelings, and I will be more sensitive next time. |
| Critic: | I don't think I want to trust you again. |
| You: | I understand how you can feel that way. I hope you will forgive me and trust me again. |

GA1139

# Game 2
# Handling Criticism by Agreeing Only!

Play the Handling Criticism Game. Read the directions and rules carefully.

Game 2:     Handling Criticism by Agreeing Only!

Directions and Rules:     You are to respond to the critic by agreeing with something that he is saying. Either agree with some grain of truth or agree in principle or agree by understanding the feelings he is having. You are not allowed to be judgmental, defensive or attacking.

After you have written your script, read aloud with your teacher and classmates. Each classmate should make a red flag. Each time a classmate hears you become defensive, attacking or judgmental, he should hold up a red flag. You must find a way ONLY to agree.

Try it. See how you like it.

Critic: You are a real cheat. I even saw you try to cheat on the homework yesterday.

You: _____

Critic: I am going to tell everyone what a cheat you are and get you back for when you accused me of cheating.

You: _____

Critic: You see you even are agreeing that you at times cheat.

You: _____

Critic: _____

You: _____

Critic: _____

You: _____

Critic: _____

    GA1139

# Game 3
# Handling Criticism the Responsible Way!

Try another Handling Criticism Game. Read the directions and rules carefully.

Game 3: Handling Criticism the Responsible Way!

Directions and Rules: Choose a classmate as a partner. Have one person be the critic and the other person be the responder. The critic writes on one of the person's papers a criticism. Then the critic hands the sheet of paper to the responder. The responder now writes a response to this criticism by the techniques learned— questioning and agreeing. Then the responder hands the sheet of paper back to the critic. The critic should respond from his own reaction. Keep passing the paper back and forth and try to avoid any red flags—attacks, judgments or defensiveness.

After the dialogue feels finished, switch. Use a new sheet of paper, but let the critic become the responder and the responder become the critic. Write a new dialogue and once again the responder must make sure to use the techniques learned— questioning and agreeing.

Use the other dialogue sheets to practice these techniques with other classmates.

After completing these dialogues with a few classmates, discuss with your teacher and classmates how it felt to be the critic. The responder. How did it feel not to be defensive, attacking or judgmental? How did it change the communication and each of your feelings? Did you allow yourself to be imperfect? Did you allow the other person to be imperfect? Were you more able to solve the problem by staying open to each other? What did you learn about yourself? About each other? What behaviors would you like to change about yourself? How will you do this? Why is agreeing and questioning a more responsible way to handle criticism? Did you help yourself maintain your self-esteem in this kind interaction? How? What rational thoughts did you use to help yourself not be self-critical?

GA1139

# Game 3 Sheet
# Handling Criticism Effectively

Critic: _____

Responder: _____

Critic: _____

Responder: _____

Critic: _____

Responder: _____

Critic: _____

Responder: _____

Critic: _____

Responder: _____

Critic: _____

Responder: _____

84

GA1139

# Game 3 Sheet
# Handling Criticism Effectively

Critic: _____

Responder: _____

Critic: _____

Responder: _____

Critic: _____

Responder: _____

Critic: _____

Responder: _____

Critic: _____

Responder: _____

Critic: _____

Responder: _____

GA1139

# Game 3 Sheet
# Handling Criticism Effectively

Critic: _____

Responder: _____

Critic: _____

Responder: _____

Critic: _____

Responder: _____

Critic: _____

Responder: _____

Critic: _____

Responder: _____

Critic: _____

Responder: _____

GA1139

# Game 3 Sheet
# Handling Criticism Effectively

Critic: _____

Responder: _____

Critic: _____

Responder: _____

Critic: _____

Responder: _____

Critic: _____

Responder: _____

Critic: _____

Responder: _____

Critic: _____

Responder: _____

GA1139

# A Parting Letter

Write yourself a letter and mail it to yourself in a few weeks. This letter will be a reminder to you of the ways in which you will help yourself to feel good always.

Dear Me,

I like myself. The things I appreciate about myself include _____

_____

_____

These are just a few appreciations. There are many more. I have learned to help myself feel good about myself by _____

_____

_____

I am taking responsibility for the way I think, feel, behave and treat others. Taking responsibility helps me to build confidence, develop self-esteem and feel good about who I am.

I value other people a great deal, and I learn to value them more as I increase my own good feelings about myself. The things I most value about others include _____

_____

_____

These are just a few appreciations. There are many more. I have learned to help others feel good about themselves by _____

_____

_____

I'm proud of myself and feel good about being responsible and thinking straight.

Lots of love,